This page is intentionally left blank.

Copyright

All rights reserved. No part of this publication may be reproduced, distributed, or transmitted in any form or by any means, including photocopying, recording, or other electronic or mechanical methods, without the prior written permission of the publisher, except in the case of brief quotations embodied in critical reviews and certain other non-commercial uses permitted by copyright law.

Get This As a FREE Audiobook via Amazon's Audible.com

Visit:
Bookskim.com/free

I'm going to show you right now a way for you to quickly create a product funnel. Period.

Obviously when I give it to you, it's going to be a very specific product funnel. Some very specific steps to take. This is designed to be a foundation. You can build on this foundation over time.

You can create additional varied types of products. Create different kinds of products, to be able to put into your funnel as time goes on. A phrased that I used in earlier teaching was this idea that, if you build your foundation correctly, and you get your foundation in place, you can literally bolt things on, just like you can bolt additional accessories onto your car. You can bold additional pieces on at will, as time goes on.

You don't want to build something that's so complex that in order to put one more piece in you've got to remake your whole business. I've seen people do that too. When they want to launch a new product, it doesn't fit with everything else. They have to remake their whole business. They go through these patterns of making sales, and remaking their business, and making sales, and remaking their business. You don't want to do that. You want to create a solid foundation. You can just literally bolt things onto the back end. Once you have this product funnel I'm going to share with you today. You've got 3, 4, 5, 6 products in the first month. Then, if you want to add another product, great! You just put it onto the end. Or, you plug it into the middle somewhere. Obviously this fits in with the automated auto responder sequences that we've been discussing. This idea that you're going to promote one product to your automated list. Through your automated e-mail campaign, for whatever the time frame is, 7, 10, 14 days. You're going to promote that.

Then, when that's over, you're going to begin to promote something else. You're going to be tracking, testing, split testing your sales page. You're going to be tracking, and testing which e-mails perform and create the most sales. As that campaign grows, say, it's got 100 e-mails in it, and you're tracking the conversion rate on each one of those e-mails, you're able to see which ones perform better than others. You can move the ones that perform better to earlier parts of the campaign, when you have higher opening click-through rates. And, over time, your conversion rates will go up, and up, and up. And, your dollars per subscriber will go up, and up, and up.

Let's talk about creating products now.

There's one assumption here that is critical. It's a critical assumption. If you're in information marketing. And, that critical assumption is that you know your topic. You know your niche.

Unfortunately, for many people, coming online. They are told that they really don't need to know very much about their niche. They can just interview experts. They can use affiliate products. They can fake it till they make it. I tend to really disagree with all of that. I believe that when you get started in information marketing the first thing that you need to do is get an education in your niche.

Obviously if your online niche is the same as your offline niche. So, if you're a doctor, or psychologist by trade, then your offline niche is medicine or psychology, then it would be real easy because you already have the knowledge.

But, if you're coming online, and you don't have any knowledge about your topic, the very first thing that you need is an education.

It's just like, you know, somebody wants to go become a dentist, they can't just hang a sign that says "Dentist", come on in, we'll try and clean your teeth, and if you have one that hurts, we'll try to rip it out. No, they're going to go and get an education.

Even if you were to decide you wanted to franchise a sandwich shop. You would have to go get an education. It might be a shorter education, but you're going to have to find out, where do I buy bread? How do we make a sandwich? What things do people like on their sandwiches? Do they like mayonnaise, or mustard, or ketchup? What kind of meats should we use? We're going to have to learn how to make a sandwich. You're going to have to learn how to bake the bread, if you're going to bake the bread. You're going to have to learn how to run the cash register. You're going to have to learn some basic marketing. Hey, are we going to send fliers out? What are we going to do?

Anytime that you start a brand new business, you have to get an eduction. I also believe that this is something the people so often leave out of information marketing. They think that, for some reason or another, they don't have to get any kind of an education. I understand why. There's so many sales pages out there that say, just use my magic system, pay me this money, fill in these blanks, and the money will just come right back to you tenfold. It's automatic, you just do this, and it happens. No education needed. You don't need to know anything.

We see this so much online. We see all of, we see so many sales letters that really focus on the fact that you don't need any education, you can be uneducated, maybe you can be illiterate, you just don't need to know anything to start an online business.

Obviously I agree with the fact that you don't need a college education. You don't have to have a certain type of a background. Unfortunately, I believe that idea of you don't need an education, that idea that you don't need to know anything, that you can start from scratch, that all you need to know how to do is turn your computer on. I believe that misleads people into believing that they don't have to have knowledge about what they're going to be teaching.

If you're in information marketing, you're teaching.

If you're teaching, you HAVE to know your material.

So, you have to have an education.

This information presupposes that you have an education in your topic, and if you don't, instead of starting a creative product, take 30 days and get an education. Go to the bookstore and buy every book on the shelf that's on your topic. Go to the library and read every book on the shelf that's on your topic. Go to Amazon.com and buy 25 books that are on your topic. And read and study them all. And, read through the bibliography and see if you can find some other books to buy and read.

Go out and buy all of your competitions products. You buy all of your competitions products and learn everything your competition knows, my guess is you'll know more than any one of your competition combined.

Let's get started on creating the actual products.

The first thing that you're going to do is, you're going to determine what I'm going to call your 6 entry products. Now, I'm using the number 6 because I believe that's a good foundational place. You can start with one product. You can start with 25. However, you don't need more than 6. You probably don't need more than 4. But, you need more than 1. You need more than 2. So, I like 6. I think if you have 6 entry level products, that you have a good foundation.

Now that might be scary, for some of you. Because, for many of you it takes 90 days to a year to create one product. So creating 6 products might take 6 years. But, not when I get done today.

We're presupposing that you know the information, and you're going to determine what are 6 topics that people need help with in your niche. If you don't know what those topics are, you go online to the various forums, you go to Yahoo Answers, you can go to Ask Jeeves, anyplace that people in your niche hang out, go in there and ask people what they're looking for. In fact, if you look for what they're already asking in those forums, you will already find out what people need that's not bing marketed correctly.

Here's the thing, if somebody's asking about it in the forum, that means they don't know where to get the information. If they don't know where to get the information, then, there's a hole. There's a vacuum that you can fill by creating a product that answers that need.

So, you're going to start out with 6 needs.

What you're going to do, is for each one of these needs, you're going to record 1 to 2 hours of information. This is going to be targeted information. It specifically targets that niche information. It specifically teaches, in the same detail that I'm teaching right here for this topic, it is going to teach your buyers exactly what they need to know. I encourage you that these 1 to 2 hour segments need to be detailed. They need to give people more information than their able to gather by surfing for free online. They need to go into detail, and they do not need to have lots of fluff.

I want to stress this because, I know in that creating a 1 to 2 hour entry level product, you're going to be maybe your competitor has a 10 hour product. But, if you buy that 10 hour product and listen to it, if it's the entry level product, you're probably going to find that there's a lot of fluff. That, out of 10 hours, there's only 1 to 2 hours of genuine information.

Now, you have a choice. You can record 10 hours of information, that's 9 hours of fluff, and 1 hour of totally solid information. Or, you can just record the 1 hour of solid information. And, my experience has been, that when people buy 1 hour of solid information, they're happier with that 1 hour of solid information, than if they by 10 hours of fluff. Because they have to take 10 hours to wade through that information.

I believe that you can create, I've done it repeatedly in the past, I've done highly concise packages that sell really well at entry price points.

Okay, so we're going to record 1 to 2 hours of each one of those products. And, the first thing that you're going to do, is you're going to outline what that product is going to be. Whatever your topic is for this particular item, for this particular recording. You're going to break it into a number of ideas or steps. You know that in a lot of my teaching, I use the number 10. The reason that I give people the number 10 is because I find that most people need a number. If you don't give them a number they get stuck on 2. A lot of times, obviously it doesn't happen with everybody. I've found if I just give people the number 10, they get to 8 and they get stuck, and that's fine. Because 8's a great number. Or they get to 10, and they might have some more, and they might write me and say can I go with 12? Well, of course you can go with 12. I want you to understand that's why I usually use the number 10, it doesn't have to be 10, it can be 6 points, it can be 8 points. I think in creating my outline for this product that I'm recording, I believe that I have about 6 points. Each one of those 6 points became a specific topic, and a specific recording.

You're going to think about what your topic is, and you're going to break it into steps. Step 1 is this, step 2 is this, step 3 is this, step 4 is this, step 5 is this, step 6 is this. You're going to write that down on a sheet of paper. Or you can type it into a Word document. Word processing document.

Then, under each one of those topics, you're going to write a synopsis of what you're going to teach. Now, that synopsis could be a list of steps to do the step. Step one might have some steps and things that you're going to teach about. It may be steps to do step 1. It may be explanation about step 1. Whatever.

You're going to write out either a synopsis, or a list of bullet points that you're going to teach from. You're going to teach when you do the recording. You're going to do this for every single one of those points. So, when you get done, you might have, and I'll be honest with you folks, I like to write this stuff out. When I teach in other places where I'm teaching, integrated article marketing and all of that, I usually have people use a word processing document. The reason for that is they can use copy and paste and use that same outline for creating multiple products. I'll be honest though, when I normally do this, I write it on a sheet of paper. The reason I write it on a sheet of paper is, it's real easy for me to edit on the fly, I don't have to have my computer open, if I'm getting ready to record, and I just want to look at those notes 5 more minutes, I can go into the pizza shop and eat some pizza, while I'm preparing for recording, and I can pull out the piece of paper, and I can say, okay, add right here. Obviously you can do that one the computer, but I find that, on the fly, boy, just writing it out makes it make a lot of sense for me.

The next step is going to be to record it. There's a few different ways that you can record. I'm not going to go into great detail on this.

The first way that you can do it, is you can literally buy an MP3 recording software for your computer if it doesn't already come with some. I'm not going to recommend any, my guess is, you've probably already got some on your computer. All you need to do is buy a microphone for your computer to do it.

There's another company that I actually use, and that's Audio Acrobat. I use Audio Acrobat, and they're literally step by step, really easy directions on Audio Acrobat. You can record by calling a certain phone number on your telephone, and they give you a pin number, and as soon as you hit the pin number, and you hit their instructions, whatever you say becomes recorded, they convert it on their software to an MP3 and a few minutes after you finish your telephone call it is loaded up and ready to go. You can literally copy and paste a link that they give you to send out and put it on your download page, and in fact I do still have download pages that still contain the Audio Acrobat original scripting that they give me rather than uploading it to my own server. Most MP3's I do upload to my own server. However, I do have content that I made, regularly make money selling, that literally has links that they give me, and they host that MP3 for me.

You can record on your computer, you can record 3-way conversations, you can record conferences, there's all kinds of things you can record using Audio Acrobat.

The service that I personally use for recording a lot of what I do because a lot of the teaching that I do is live teaching, and I'll invite someone to participate with me, so that I can get feedback. The reason I like feedback when I'm teaching, because it's not necessary. The reason I like feedback when I'm teaching is, if for some reason if what I'm teaching doesn't make sense, some part of it doesn't make sense, the person that's on the phone with me, can ask me, hey, what does that mean? Can you tell me more about that? I'm confused.

They're confused, then a lot of other people might be confused. I'm able to answer that question. You don't need that element when you're recording these entry level items. What will happen is, when you sell it the first time, you will get e-mails with people asking you the same questions. All you do is take all their questions and answer them for them as they send them to you in e-mail, take all their questions, and at the end of the week, after you've made 10 sales, or 20 sales, or 100 sales, whatever. You simply take all the peoples questions and record a Q&A recording, and just add it to the download page, so that all future buyers will get the add-on information.

Does that make sense?

[Other Voice] Yes

Excellent, thank you. The software that I personally use to these types of 3-way conversations is Instant Teleseminar which is a product put out by Xiosoft.com. There are plenty of other services that will do the same thing, in fact, I'm not even recommending, or not recommending either one of these services, I'm simply indicating that that's what I use. I don't know if either one of these are the best on the market. I use them. I like them. They work really well for me. I understand them. I don't have to learn new software.

You know, every once in awhile you get somebody who wants to recommend something that's better than what you have already. For me the opportunity cost of learning a new type of software, is much greater than simply going along with what I already love. Okay, so, if you've got something that you like better. By all means, use that.

I use this process, or a very similar process, to create almost all, or probably now all of my entry level products. Now, I've told you it's 1 to 2 hours worth of content. What I like to do is to break that content up into recordings on each of those particular topics. Okay, so, if you've got the 6 topics. I like to have 6 recordings. Now, these recordings don't need to be any particular length. They need to be exactly as long as is necessary to teach that topic. So, one topic takes 10 minutes, that's a 10 minute recording. If another topic takes 2 hours, then that's a 2 hour recording.

This allows a couple of things to happen. One of the things that happens is, the person wants to learn and listen, they want to skip ahead to a particular topic, they can easily do it, simply by selecting the audio for whatever the particular topic is that they want to learn.

And, no really, that's the biggest thing. Is that people are able to do that. And, if they're going through just sequentially, starting at the beginning, they can maybe listen to one recording a day, over the course of 6 days, rather than having to listen to a full 2 hour recording all in one sitting. And, maybe missing some of what's going on. I just find that that's a really convenient way to do it.

I really want to stress this idea that if you've done Step 1, which is you know your material. Creating the outline takes maybe half an hour. Literally, half an hour. Now, the first one might take a little bit longer. But, you're literally making a very basic outline that you're going to teach from. The actual recording of 2 hours worth of information, takes exactly 2 hours. If you're recording 1 hour of information, it takes 1 hour. If you're recording 3 hours of information, it takes 3 hours.

Then there's something literally if you create a 2 hour product, maybe it has 4 half our recordings on it. That teach specifically, exactly, what it is that you're teaching. Then, that's your introductory product, it takes you 2 hours to create, a half an hour for outline, 2 and a half hours. Many of you could create one product a day, for the next 6 days, and have your 6 products created. Or, you could create 1 product a week, for the next 6 weeks, and have your 6 products created.

Obviously, having 6 products is nice for a couple of different reasons. Number 1, it gives you several entry points, where people can come in to one particular product and eventually be up-sold to the other 5 products. The second thing that it does is, it allows you to have 6 products to market to someone new that comes onto your list. Say, they don't buy product #1, now you expose them to product #2. They don't buy product #3, you expose them to product #4.

Any questions on this process of creating an entry level product to sell to your list?

[Elaine] I have a question Sean.

[Sean] Sure, go ahead Elaine.

[Elaine] If we're using this method to create an entry level product, and we wanted to create an e-book, what we would have to do is to send the MP3 to get transcribed, and produce the e-book in that method. In that way, wouldn't we?

[Sean] Yes, we certainly could do that. Yes, we certainly could do that. Then we could use that transcription, we could clean it up, we could probably make the e-book even more concise. Because, if you think about the piece I've been doing now, for what?, the last 15 or 20 minutes, there's been a little bit of explanation that might be duplicated from one of the other recordings. So, if you're putting all of this into an e-book you could take that particular information out.

I'll tell you why, though, that I'm not too fond of using this as an e-book. And that is because the e-book generally commands a lower price, just because it's an e-book. The problem is, that I believe you should be selling your information based on what it's worth, and what the value is to the buyer for the information, not the number of words, or not the number of hours. This is something that I've really been building into, and working on, in my business. It's so easy to price according to how many recordings there are, or how many pages there are. But really, things should not be priced that way. They should priced based on a value that they deliver.

So, if you've got an MP3 that has a value of $200, let's say. That means that the value of the information in it is $200. Well, if you break that down into an e-book, and the same information is in the e-book, it's just in written form. You'll have a really hard time selling that $197, when you have the MP3's with the same information for $197. In fact, it really should not be sold for less than $197, if that's what the market will bear for that particular information.

I really shy away from doing that.

Now, is that something that you could use to create some partial, give-away e-books, you know, maybe take 10 minutes worth of your recording and make that into a give-away e-book? Yes, absolutely. You certainly could do that. Could you take that MP3 information, have it transcribed, and then make 400 word articles out of it? Yes, absolutely. And, to be truthful with you, you're right, you could create the e-book from it. I just don't see that in today's market, as being the greatest strategy. I just don't see that as being the greatest strategy in today's market. Does that make sense?

[Elaine] Yes it does, and based on what you just said, could I, if I wanted to, not go MP3's, but go with CD's? So if someone knew the prices, I'll send them an MP3, but in the post would be 2 sets of CD's which will give more value.

[Sean] You can certainly sell CD's, instead of MP3's. However, I'm finding in my testing that conversion rates aren't any higher for the physical product. In fact, I'm finding that sometimes an MP3 converts at a higher conversion rate than the CD. And, if that's the case, then why create the physical product if, and there's obviously. Let me rephrase what I've just said.

There's lots of good reasons to create the physical product. However, if we're just talking about an entry level sale, I believe that conversion rates are the same, if not higher, with MP3's for that first initial sale. I'll tell you a place where CD's, the physical product is really helpful is in creating long term value. And in creating, getting people to the place where they do trust you more. And, they look to you as the trusted adviser, the trusted expert. I believe that a great place to do that is on your 2nd product that someone buys, not your first one.

Obviously, that can be argued all over the place, but here's the thing. If somebody's looking at your entry level product, they have a problem, and they need an answer NOW. Not 5 days later when your package gets to them. Does that make sense?

[Elaine] Yeah. And that answers my question, and I'm [interrupting] in what direction I need to go.

[Sean] Okay, excellent. Folks, any other questions on these entry level products?

Okay, if there aren't any other questions, let's move on to creating your first up-sell. Okay, now I want to explain up-sell here. The common language that folks use now in the internet marketing niche, internet marketing world is that an up-sell is something that, if someone purchases product 1 from you, then as soon as they buy it, they have an opportunity on the download page, or the thank you page, or on a one-time offer page to buy the up-sell. That's a great place to create some more revenue right now.

However, I'm not fully convinced, after lots of testing. I'm not fully convinced that that's the way to maximize total revenue through the lifetime of the customer. Is it a way to bump an extra 20% today? If you have 10 people buy a $100 product, so it's $1k, and you get 2 of them to buy another $100 product, let's just say for example on an average. You know, you add another 20% of revenue. Can you create nice up-sell streams that you create 50%, or even 100% of additional revenue right there on the up-sell? Yeah. Yeah, in many niche's you can. So, you double the $1k, to $2k, right there on the spot.

However, my experience is that if you don't up-sell these individuals, then a week or two later, they'll spend the same money they would have spent with you right there on the up-sell page. That's my experience. They'll spend just as much with you a week later as they would have right away. And, we know that, and I think we have to be careful here because, sometimes we're talking about a marketer that doesn't really work a whole lot on trust and relationship, they just want to make the sales. And, that's okay.

But, in my business, I'm big on the trust and relationship. I don't want people who just buy one product from me. I really don't! I mean, sure, the extra $97 is nice, but that's not what I'm looking for. I'm looking for the person who's going to buy from me once and study it, and say, "Wow, this is great information. I'd like to get more from Sean." And, they go out and buy something else.

And a month later they say, "Boy, that was great! I used it, and it helped my business, I'm going to come back to Sean." And they buy something else. I want people who are going to buy something from me every single month, for 3 years. And, continue to create great value.

I want to build that relationship. I believe that those instant up-sells, I don't have proof of this, but I just believe that those instant up-sells pull away from that. I work so hard for 14 days when somebody comes into my campaign to get them to make a, I'm not even trying to get them to make a purchase. Especially the first 5 to 7 days. All I want to do is to trust me. That's it! I want to give them competent information, I want people to trust me. I want them to already use something that I give them for free. And, have some results in their business. Then, when they buy the first product, to me that's not an opportunity, oh, I could make it into one, but I don't believe that should just be an opportunity to sell them as much as possible. I think that should be an opportunity to over deliver. So that they are building on the trust that they've already established with me. So that now their trust grows. And, they'll buy more in the future.

Now, that's just my personal theory. Obviously, split test it in your own lists. See, do you make more revenue by doing an instant up-sell, or do you make more revenue by waiting 10 days. You know, where do you make the most revenue? Where do you make the most revenue 3 years from now? Here's the thing, I know a lot of people when they're first starting out, they don't care about their revenue 3 years from now. Because, they don't have any idea what that might look like. But, for me, I have people on my list that have been buying from me for years now. I mean, literally, right now today as I record this, there's people who have bought from me for 4 years. Literally, for 4 years. And, still trust me to buy the next thing that comes out.

Now, for me, when I make a sale today, I'm not interested in the quick buck that I'm going to get by making that quick up-sell happen. Folks, that's not to say that from time to time, if an up-sell is appropriate, if everything looks good, that I'm not going to offer an up-sell from time to time. In terms of just making it the standard thing that I do all the time, I believe that he value, the total customer value, possibly can be higher, by not focusing so much on that. So, bit of a rabbit trail I just went down there. This was not in my outline notes, I'll give it to you extra so, let's call that a bonus.

When I'm talking about an up-sell. I'm thinking about up-selling someone after they have had time to consume the information. So they purchase a $97 item, and they use it, they consume it. They begin to use it. They begin to get results. Then, 7 to 10 days later, I can offer them something that is a much higher ticket item than that first, initial item. Then, there's a great chance that they're going to make that purchase. In fact, they'll invest more with me after 7 to 10 days, than they would have invested on the up-sell. What this does is this gives me an opportunity to market a $2k coaching program. Or a $1k home-study course.

The psychology here is, let's say, 10 topics in your niche that someone could learn about. And, really, they could learn about all 10 of these topics. Now, they could learn 1 topic from you. One topic from your competition. One topic from their competition. And literally buy products to learn from 10 different people.

What's probably going to happen is, they're not going to like everybody's teaching style. Some people like my teaching style, some people probably don't like my teaching style. Now, that's okay! Because, the people that do, buy from me. And, the people that don't, it's okay. They'll buy from my competition, and, that'll work. Because, that's the right teaching style for them.

If someone buys your initial product. Let's say it's a $97 2hr recording. They like it! They got great value! They were really excited about the fact that it was 2hrs instead of 10 for the exact same content. They learned a lot. They were able to go out and implement it immediately.

And, 7 to 10 days down the road their thinking, I need more information on this topic. I want to do more. And, maybe their looking at your competition. And now you offer them a complete home study course that contains advanced information on all 10 topics that they need. Because of the fact that they've just purchased from you, and they like what they've gotten from you. That makes them likely to be open to purchasing your much larger program than they would have been willing to trust you to provide on the up-sell.

Because, remember, they were buying a $97 product because that's what they trusted you, to be able to purchase from you. Until they consume that, their trust hasn't grown. Sure, there's some psychological evidence, I mean, there is psychological evidence that shows that somebody's got their wallet open, and they make 1 purchase, then a percentage of them will make the 2nd purchase. Again, going back to the psychology, I'm really leaning towards you lose more in trust than you gain in total revenue over the life of the customer. What I'm concerned with is that life of the customer. And, so, we've got this $997 product perhaps, that we're going to offer 7-10 days later.

Now, this is going to be the up-sell. It's going to happen, instead of the download page, the thank you page, it's going to happen 7-10 days later in your campaign.

Before I teach on how you're going to create this home study course, I want you to remember what I talked about earlier about building your foundation when you're creating your products. You're building your initial foundation of 6 products. And, in fact, you don't even need all 6 before you can start selling. You start by selling #1 as soon as you create it. And, next week, when you release product #2, when you create product #2, and you release it to your list, more people will buy product #2, some of the people who bought product #1 might buy product #2. Then week 3, you release something else, you sell that to your list, people who've bought nothing, might by this. Some people who bought product #1 might buy this. Some people who bought product #2, might buy product #3. And so on, you're just adding that new product on, and you're putting it in your auto-responder as I taught in the last teaching. You're simply putting that into the auto-responder.

Okay, so you don't have to start out with this up-sell. However, once you've created those 6 products, now you go out and create your complete home study course for example. Now let's just the $997 number. Okay, now, if you start out with a $97 entry level product, I find that $997 is a good multiple for that 2nd product.

If you start out, let's say, a $500 product. Then, what you may want to do, is go with instead, a $2k product for your 2nd product. That would be a multiple of 4. You could probably even go with a $5k product. Which would be the full multiple of 10. For that 2nd product. So, somewhere between a multiple of 4 and 10 for the 2nd product.

The way that you are going to be at ... let's talk about 2 things. We'll talk about first about the relation of that $997 product. Then we'll talk about the psychology of capturing as many sales as possible. So, let's talk about the creation of that product. We're going to make this fast, and the reason that we can make this fast is, because we're going to use the exact ... same ... process. For creating our 10hr program, that's $997 in this example, as we used to create our 1 to 2 hour program that was $97.

Okay, we're going to determine what our topics are. Let's say these are more advanced topics, we're going to list out all of these topics, we're going to have 10 main topics, for example. Then we're going to have some ideas that we're going to share during each one of those hours. We're going to write those out.

Or, we're going to type those into a word document. And, we're going to record this, 1hr at a time.

Okay, and the reason that I stress this record this 1 hour at a time is, you know, a lot of people will put off creating something like this is because it's going to take 10 hours of recording. You don't have 10hrs today! And, you probably won't have 10hrs tomorrow. You won't have 10hrs the next day. But, if you were really serious about creating a coaching, or a complete home study course, could you not set aside ONE hour a day for 10 days, once you've written the outline, just record 1hr every single day for 10 days. And, in 2 weeks, you would have a complete home study course that you could offer on the back end.

Now remember, you're not offering it until 7 - 10 days after somebody's made the 1st purchase anyway! So, this is something, literally, if you were to record 1hr a day, you could create, let's say, you even had 2hr products at the beginning, 1 hr a day. It would take you 12 days, to create your first 6 products. Then it would take you another 10 days to create your home study course. 22 days! And you would have your 6 products, plus your home study course.

Not everybody is going to purchase the $997 home study course. At first blush. So, let's say that we use our automated campaign to market to these individuals for 3 days in a row, the $997 course, and we have a percentage of people who purchase it. You know, 1% purchase it. 3% purchase. Remember, these are buyers, it's only being promoted to people who bought the earlier purchase. So, they go through 3 days at $997, maybe we give them a break for a day or two. Now we come back with a payment offer. Perhaps $997 was too much right now, however, we can split this into 3 payments at $337. And, what we will find is, whatever conversion rate that we were able to make on the first $997, we will find that that many people again will purchase at the payment rate.

You might ask, why not start with payments? Well, because if we start with payments, in the total number of sales, what I believe that we see is in the tests that we do. Is that we don't get as many total sales, if we start out with that $337 number. And the reason for that is, that people initially assign value to something based on the first price that they seriously consider purchasing the item at. So, if they initially consider purchasing something at $997, they're going to assign more value to it than the $337 payment. This allows us to capture those individuals who are going to pay the full $997 right up front. It allows us to cement in peoples minds, this is worth $997. And then when we make a 3 payments of $337 offer, people feel like they're getting a great value for their money because their able to begin studying for $337.

Now, we could take this to the next step and come up with a, after 3 to 5 additional days, we could come up with another payment price that we could put in there. So, we might have 10 payments of $97, or 12 payments of $97. Or, we could drop down now to a lower priced home study course. Now, this could be a portion of your big home study course. Half of the big home study course. You could break your big home study course down into 2 segments of part 1 and part B. You could offer them, you know, you don't want to invest $997, or 3 payments of $337, for the entire program. But I've put together a special offer for you today, and this is part 1 of the program, you purchase that today for $497. And, when you've completed part 1, if you wish to purchase part 2 you can. I'll give you a great deal on it. But, if you don't, and all you need is part 1, then that's okay. And, some people will purchase at $497. And, remember, we're automating all of this in our automated campaign. And, 3-5 days after they've had the opportunity to purchase at $497, now maybe they have an opportunity to purchase at 3 payments of $170. 5 days later they have an opportunity to purchase at 5 payments of $97. You can even take this to the extreme and do 10 payments of $57. What you're doing is you're allowing yourself to sell, at a fair price, because the price really is the same to everybody that purchases it. You're allowing people to purchase this at a payment price that works for them. Obviously, the person who's paying $57 a month, they're going to pay the same thing, or maybe even a little bit more at the end of the payment term. However, they're able to make that payment in chunks, in payments, that makes sense for them. Because, that's what they're able to afford.

This process allows us to find out, what's the highest price that someone's able to afford to make purchases. If we were to start out at say 10 payments of $570, instead of, of $497, then a lot of people might opt for the payments of $57, that would have been willing to make the full payment earlier. Now, in the long run, your cash flow is probably going to be a little bit less on the payment, because probably not everybody makes all of the payments. So, certainly that is factored in. The biggest difference here is that if someone makes that $997 purchase, then the money has already been invested. We can do the same thing 7 - 10 days after that purchase, and up-sell to something else.

Whereas, if somebody goes onto a payment plan of 10 payments of $57, you're not going to be able to up-sell them to a $3k package 7 - 10 days later. You might be able to up-sell them into $97 / month payments or something like that. What this allows us to do, is use this as a filter to determine at what price point individuals are willing to pay. That are on our list. And, based on their willingness and ability to pay, we can offer products and services that fit into their needs and their price point.

I'm going to give you another way that you can create your $997 home study course.

Another way that you can create your $997 home study course, let's say that it's going to have 10 lessons. Or, 10 recordings. You could sell it as a 10 week coaching program. The delivery information will be exactly the same on each one of those 1hr segments. But, instead of recording those segments, let's say, in your home office. Or, in your spare bedroom. By yourself. Or, with one other person on the call. Instead, you would record each one of those sessions as a live coaching session. Where you could have your coaching clients speak up and ask questions. Okay, at the end of 10 weeks you would have a 10 hour home study course. So, you simply take the recordings from that coaching program, and put those recordings into, package those up, so that it becomes a home study course.

Obviously, the primary product creating information that I'm giving you here is about simply sitting down and recording those as quickly as possible. I go into great depth in my coaching program course on literally hours of content on how to launch a 10 week coaching program. Just like what I've discussed, you don't need to do that any way shape or form. You can literally record it the way that I've taught you. But, I did have that in my notes, and I wanted to share that with you as an option. As an idea. Especially for those of you that perhaps already have a coaching program.

Let's talk about creating a sales letter for your product. When you're first starting out, you don't know how to write a sales letter. If you're just starting out, you don't know how to create a product, but I've just taught you how to do it. Literally, step by step, exactly how to do it.

Creating a product is something that I can teach in half an hour, 45 minutes. Those are literally the steps, I've given you those steps. However, to learn to write a good, compelling sales letter. Could take 3 months, 6 months, a year. Many people it takes 5 years, before they get to the place where they can write a nice, compelling sales letter. I say 5 years, or 3 years. I mean, of the work. Learning how to write the words. Learning what to write. Learning how to write it. Obviously, if your background is in some other type of sales, then, hey, writing a sales letter is going to be a lot easier.

What I find, is the very easiest thing for beginners to do when they are creating their initial products, is to not try to write their own sales letter. Instead, to use sales letter software. I'm going to give you a couple of suggestions right here for which ones I recommend. That I've used, and my clients have used. In the growing process.

One of the big core arguments here for people is, it won't say exactly what I want it to say. It won't tell them all about my product. These sales letter softwares will be able to tell them as much as you want. Because, you can certainly customize all of the language. But one of the things that I find that beginners do is in writing sales letters, is they spend far too much time telling all about their product instead of all the other things that a sales letter should do.

My experience has shown that your time is far better spent creating one more product than learning how to write a sales letter your first month. Now, I want to be clear. If you're going to make a full time living in information marketing, or you're going to make more than a full time living in information marketing. At some point you need to learn to write good copy. Now, I really believe that. Even if you're going to outsource everything that you do, I really believe personally need to learn to write good copy. Even if you're not going to write most of your copy. If you know how to do it, then you can evaluate copy that somebody does for you. You hire a copy writer to write copy for you, go and read it. Evaluate it. You won't be able to do that if you don't know it. So, in the long run I believe that you need to learn to write copy.

In the short run though, and that's what this is about, because you want to get these products out fast. I believe you should use sales letter software.

One way to find that software is you just Google "Sales Letter Software". I don't recommend doing that. Because there's a LOT of software out there now, that just is basically fill in the blanks, headlines, and all the different sections, and it just pretty much uses, in my experience, just standard sales phrases and you fill in a lot of your own material and I just don't like the way that a lot of that software looks.

So, I'm going to recommend a couple that I believe very strongly in. And that is Brett McFall's sales letter software. I don't have a link for you, you literally Google Brett McFalls.

And then, Marlin Sanders, has an excellent, I have a client who used this and created an excellent sales letter. Marlin Sanders has an excellent sales letter software.

Those are the two I recommend, certainly there's some other good ones out there, these are the two that I've personally had experience with.

When I first got started, I wrote a lot of sales letters that converted really well with Brett McFalls software. I don't believe I've used Malin's, I may own Marlin's, but I don't know that I've ever used it. I have seen the work that it produces, recently a client created a beautiful sales letter using that software. That's what I recommend.

Now, for LONG TERM, learning to write your own sales letters. I recommend to go to the copy writing masters. I really do. I recommend finding copy writing masters, and studying. I'm not going to recommend any one particular person here. I don't believe that the best way for you to learn copy writing is to just study from one person. I really believe you need to take multiple courses, study the great sales letters out there, and practice writing copy, practice, practice, practice. Working it all together. I don't believe there's a one size fits all, learn in 90 days, how to write great sales letters, that do a great job of persuasion.

This is a belief. That's my belief. Two places that I get that belief. #1 is my own personal experience. #2 is watching other people as they progress in their sales letter writing. The people that perform the very best. If you look at the great copy writers. So many have studied from so many different places, so much trial and error. And, that's how they've done it.

So, in short, use sales letter software. I recommend Brett McFalls, or Marlin Sanders.

There's one other type of sales page that has become pretty popular recently and that is the video sales page, and a lot of folks are using the video sales page. They claim higher conversion rates with the video sales page. One thing that's beautiful about a video sales page is it doesn't take as much time to create.

If you want to create something yourself. However, there is a formula that needs to be followed to make that happen. There's a few different folks out there that are teaching that process now. I believe that the place where you can probably get the best information on that is from Ryan Deiss at http://www.digitalmarketer.com/video-salesletter-formula-report/, and he includes a tutorial there on creating video sales pages. How to design the powerful information and then how to deliver it and what to put into it.

Again, a video sales page is not necessary, and there are some other companies / people out there that are promoting it. However, I know that Ryan Deiss includes that information. It should be real good, solid information for you.

Moving on, let's discuss one more up-sell that you could put into a complete funnel. Obviously, this is about creating a [garbled] and we've talked about two places there, two items that you would put into the complete funnel. The first one is, a product, 1 - 2 hour initial entry product. And then the 2nd is a home study course, $997, 10 CD home study course. Or half of that, or part 1 for $497, with some payment options.

Another thing that you can add onto your complete funnel, very, very quickly, is a coaching program. Now, I teach this in my how to sell coaching programs program. So, we're not going to go into great detail on this here. Because the detail is there. And, you don't need this. You do not need this to create your product funnel. You'll be able to create all if it with what I've just shared with you. 1 - 2 hours of your entry level products, 10 hour CD's for $997, then 5 hours for $497 product.

However, if you want to add on a coaching program, it's relatively easy to do. In fact it's very easy to do. You don't even really need a sales page for a coaching program, if you're making sales. Because, what happens is, people who buy from you, a percentage of them naturally are looking for coaching from you. You can go anywhere from creating the highest level, a complete sales letter to sell the coaching, all the way down to literally just sending an e-mail out to your list asking people if they're interested in doing some coaching with you. When they write you back, you ask them what they need help with, you tell them what you're able to help them with, you talk about, in these e-mails going back and forth, you simply talk about the value that somebody will be able to get out of it. They'll ask you questions, you'll share the price of your coaching with them. And, they'll either sign up, or they won't. It can be as simple as that. Or, it can be as complex as writing a sales letter for the coaching program.

So, let's talk about somebody coming into your coaching program. The first person that comes into your coaching program, you are going to write your lessons based on that particular person's needs. So, lesson 1, is something that this person needs. Lesson 2, is something that this person needs. Lesson 3, is something that this person needs. As you create those lessons you're going to put them into an auto-responder so that anybody in the future that needs a similar coaching to what person #1 wanted. You will not have to create fresh lessons, you'll simply put them into the same auto-responder sequence that you took the first client through.

Now, if person #2 comes along, and has a different set of needs, there's 2 things that you can do. #1, you could create a 2nd set of lessons for that person, then in the future you've got 2 options for people with 2 types of needs that people can fit into. OR! What I recommend is taking the 1st set of lessons, having your 2nd client go through the 1st set of lessons, I'm assuming that they're similarly niched, they should be. If you're selling products that are similarly niched, your coaching should be similarly niched. And then go in and add to each lesson what's necessary for client #2. When client #3 comes in, go in and add to the lessons what's necessary for client #3. Once you've got through 5 - 10 clients, you'll have everything that almost anybody needs. If somebody needs something that's not on these lessons, after 10 clients. You're probably looking at somebody that needs something different than you're really all about anyhow, and that's when you turn the coaching down. You say, you know what, you find out what their needs are, you find out that you can't help them, and you let them know, look, I can't help you. I don't teach on that particular topic, or you could make the decision to create a new coaching program. Or, continue to add information to the prior.

This makes it very, very easy to sell coaching, you can literally sell it before you create it. In fact, it's impossible, to create the first, in my opinion, it's impossible to create a perfect round of coaching lessons before people purchase anyhow. Because, even after someone purchases, and you create lessons that work, you're still going to need to make adjustments, until you find out what all of the needs, specific needs, and questions are in your niche. It's different than creating a product, because with a coaching program, people have questions. That's the whole basis of the coaching program. It's the fact that they can ask questions. That's the biggest difference between a coaching program and just the material.

A product is just the material. Coaching is the material, plus, the ability to ask questions.

Okay folks, let's open up and see if there's questions or comments on anything that I've covered here about creating your product funnel, and creating it quickly.

[Leonardo] Going back to where you said create part 1 for half the money. If someone buys that, would you then add in at the end of the follow up for that product, the 2nd half?

[Sean] For them to purchase?

[Leonardo] Yeah, so, if they buy the part 1 for $497, do you later on offer them part 2?

[Sean] Yes! If they purchase it, they will get offered part 2 later on. Okay, now, the timing may not be exactly the same. Depending on how the material is presented. However, if it's all on one download page. And there's 5 hours of content. I would go with the same formulas, 7 - 10 days. They've experienced part 1, now here's this opportunity to purchase part 2 for an additional $497.

Okay, now what you could do, if you're planning this as your strategy, you could offer part 1 for $597, instead of $497, then you could offer part 2 at a $200 discount for $397. Your total revenue would be the same. Within a few dollars. If we're rounding 7's you would be at $994, if they purchase the first part at $597, and the 2nd part at $397 which would be a $200 discount. Does that make sense?

[Leonardo] Yeah, that makes sense.

When you're offering the $997, are you comfortable offering just the same price split between 3 payments?

[Sean] Yes, I'm completely comfortable with that, I'm completely comfortable with that. I do recognize I'm not going to get every single payment. I'm going to get most payments, but I'm not going to get every single payment. It just happens that way, people. You've got to understand, if somebody takes your payment option, the reason they didn't pay you the full $997, is usually because they don't have $997 on their credit card. Okay, that's the biggest reason. Sometimes it's because they don't trust you enough, but if you do the kind of marketing that I do with trust at the front end, and they buy a product and have 7 - 10 days to consume it, they like it, they trust you. In my opinion, the biggest reason that they take a payment option is because they simply do not have $997 in the bank. But they do have $335. Okay, now, if they don't have $997 in the bank, then they're pretty much spending what they take in every month. Okay, economically, that's what's happening to that person.

They full well intend to make payment #2 and payment #3. Let's say month 2 comes along and they barely have enough money to pay you, but the payment's coming through, they'll make it happen. Month #3 comes along, they've already scrunched in month #2 to try to make sure the money's there, and when the month 3 comes along it's just not there. The payment's going to fail.

Okay, now, a lot of times, if you write that person and say, hey, I noticed that the payment failed, how's things going with the product? They tell you that things are going well, and they're really sorry they couldn't make that payment. You just ask the, you say let me ask you this, John, it's $335, what if I split that into 4 payments, we'll do $87 / month for the next 4 months, would that be okay with you?

You know, what I've found is most people will say, yeah, that'll be great. Thanks for working with me. It's not that they don't want you to get paid, it's that the reason that they took payments in the first place, is because they have a finance challenge. If you make it now more affordable for them to make the last payment, they'll make it for you. Now, I've done that before, repeatedly in the past. Where I've refinanced my financing with somebody, because something happens. You simply have to recognize this. Sometimes that won't work. They just don't have the money. Something happened, they thought they were going to have the money, they don't have it. So, you aren't going to make quite as much on your payments.

But, remember this! They weren't going to buy in the first place. So, whatever payments they make, is additional revenue for you, because it's a digital product, it doesn't cost you anything else to allow one additional person to purchase that product. Right?

[Leonardo] Absolutely, yeah.

[Sean] Even if everybody only made 2 payments, then you would still be ahead of not giving that payment plan at all.

[Leonardo] And the people who bought it for $997, they wouldn't see that payment plan anyway, would they, because they would have been moved off of that list.

[Sean] Well, they should not, however, you always want to make sure that you never do anything that's unethical or that people, if they did find out about it would have a problem. I mean, if somebody paid $997, and saw that now there's a payment option for $337, you know, 9 times out of 10. I mean, obviously, the payments are the same, the payments are the same, so it's not like they were cheated by paying a higher price. They simply didn't have the opportunity to finance it, but remember, they paid the payment, so if they don't have the money they financed it probably on a credit card anyway, so to them, it's no different. They're going to make the same credit card payment every month as if they were to make you monthly payments, by breaking it down.

Now, that's another value of having a higher price for monthly payments. I think most marketers do a higher price for monthly payments. It helps you cover the fact that you don't get all of your payments, all of the time. It also makes it more reasonable for that client that does pay full price, that the incentive to pay full price is that it's really a lower price. I mean, really, it's $997 if you pay for it in full, but if you make payments, it's going to end up being $1150 or $1200. Does that make sense?

[Leonardo] Yes, so instead of the 3 payments at $337, they could be at $377, or whatever.

[Sean] Yeah, absolutely.

Yeah, something should be there that there's a bit of a premium on it. That's my opinion on it, I believe if you put a bit of a premium on it. You know, if you're just looking for $, split test it. Everything you do should go into a split tester. So, you could split test what's the conversion rate between $337 and $377. 3 payments of $337 and 3 payments of $377, what's the conversion rate? Is there a significant difference? Well, if there is, maybe you go with $337. Split test that vs. 4 payments of $250, what worked better? 5 payments of $197. I have this set up so that, I mean, the key here is that, and I see so many marketers, they want to do all of this at one time, they want to have a $997 offer, and a 3 times $337, and a 10 times $120, and then people choose one of the three.

I personally believe that total conversion rates, over a week or two, I don't have to get paid today, doesn't make any difference to me if I get paid today, or in 7 days. I don't care if somebody buys today, or in 7 days. Doesn't matter to me, the money's going to spend exactly the same when I get it. I don't care if somebody buys today if they're just going to buy in 7 days. Doesn't make any difference.

Okay, now, if they're not going to buy in 7 days, yeah, I want them to buy today. Okay, but if we have multiple opportunities for people to maximize the people that will buy at $997, maximize the number of people who'll by at 3 payments, maximize the people that'll buy at 10 payments, maximize the people at $497, maximize the people at 3 @ $170, maximize the people at 5 @ $97, then I'm able to generate the maximum number of sales in 21 days, instead of the minimum number of sales all on day 1. And, I would rather take the maximum number of sales, spilled out over 21 days, than the minimum number of sales, spread out over 3 days. Can you see that?

[Leonardo] Yes. Absolutely, yeah.

[Sean] Excellent

[Leonardo] Thanks

[Sean] You're welcome.

Any other questions on anything I've taught here?

[Jeff] Yeah, this is Jeff, I have 2.

Okay, the first one, you and I have been e-mailing back and forth since the class a week or two ago. I started with the funnels. I'm not sure if I have more entry level products than I think I have. What I was trying to do was create funnels from what I already have, and put more spokes in the fire out there as entry level things. Based on what you taught on today, I'm not sure the things all work together where they all go to a home study course. I guess my first question is, do your 6 entry level products all point to the same up-sell home study, next level? Do they all point in that direction?

[Sean] Well Jeff, long term, they don't have to. Keep in mind that what I've just taught is giving the concept that somebody can start from zero, and create 6 products in a couple of weeks, and create a home study course that goes along with that. In your case, you've already got products, you may find that you've got 3 entry level products that really fit with one home study course, you've got 4 that fit with a different one, 6 others that fit with a 3rd one. But in your case, you would have multiple back ends. Absolutely, but really the model that I've given here, again, it's an expandable model, this is simply the foundation, you could bolt onto the back of it as much as possible. This is not designed to be, this is exactly the way that it has to be done. This is more designed as this is one way you can get this done, really, really, quickly. So that you have a foundation, so that you can begin to plug other things into the back of it and add to it over time.

[Jeff] I think what I did was, I was thinking very linearly when it came to these funnels. And, I linked up a free report to an entry level product, and then that led to it's own up-sell. And, things like that. And I ended up with 13 linear funnels, but I think that I can actually spread that out some more so that many more all go into the same up-sell, so I can actually spend more time creating my up-sell products, because I have like I said, I believe I have more entry level products at different price points than I thought I had. So, that's question #1. Now I can't remember what question #2 was.

You were just talking about it with Leonardo. I don't know, if it comes up again, I'll bring it up. But, that answers one of my questions.

[Sean] Alright, sounds good Jeff. Sounds good. Any other questions or comments specifically on this product creation process. I'll open things up for other questions in just a moment. Any other questions on this product creation process?

www.ingramcontent.com/pod-product-compliance
Lightning Source LLC
Chambersburg PA
CBHW071241220526
45468CB00002B/951